I0436956

The New Edition: The Truth

A Way Out of the Wilderness:
Muslim Views during the
Election of 2008

Wazhma Khalili

Order this book online at www.trafford.com
or email orders@trafford.com

Most Trafford titles are also available at major online book retailers.

Printed in the United States of America.

ISBN: 978-1-4269-4290-7 (sc)
ISBN: 978-1-4269-4291-4 (e)

Trafford rev. 04/29/2011

 www.trafford.com

North America & international
toll-free: 1 888 232 4444 (USA & Canada)
phone: 250 383 6864 ♦ fax: 812 355 4082

Books by this author;

Rough Road;
The Public Administration Exists in name only in
Afghanistan

The Truth;
A Way Out of the Wilderness:
Muslim-Views during the Election of 2008

ISBN: 1-4392-3236-9

ISBN-13:   9781439232361

BookSurge

Please feel free to voice your opinion and learn
more about the author at her website;
www.wazhmathetruth.com

Dedication

I would like to dedicate this new edition of my first book, to my respected and adorable parents. To my remarkable dad Motasimbilla Khalili, my outstanding mother Alia Khalili and my little love, my precious child, Sarah Khalili Khan. They have all been there for me and supported me throughout my education. Each one of you means the world to me. I love you all from the bottom of my heart.

Thank you to Al-Underwood My

Best Friend

Al Underwood

Thank you for offering to help me with editing my book for me and supporting me with this book. Thanks for your friendship and for your kindness once again, for standing by me to help me be successful.

Contents

Foreword

In this book, I will examine several main points of discriminations, racism, and sexism. I will show you why I believe the President Obama will take an action to stop all this discriminations. We all see and believe that U.S. is a demarcating country, and we all should work together to stop this power of Abuse.

The Truth - A Way out of the Wilderness: Muslim Views During the Election of 2008

Introduction:

Muslims in the U.S. had many of the same concerns as other Americans: patriotism, the federal budget, and the economy. However, as far as elections were concerned, many Muslims feel they had only a small influence over American foreign policy (Pew Research Center, 2007).

As all citizens are, challenged to participate in the political system process, in my experience, Muslim Americans behave as Americans, in spite of what the polls say, or what people tend to think about them as a religious entity. Some Muslims in America felt that they were, misjudged, despite the content of their hearts and their true character. Indeed, many Muslim Americans believe that the main problem today is discrimination based on their ethnicity and religion. For example, it is certainly amazing that a black man with a Muslim sounding name and Muslim parentage was the Democratic frontrunner for the US presidential election in 2008. U.S. President Barack Obama, an African American Christian, was facing questions about his Muslim roots.

In other words, he might not get a fair chance, in the general election, because of his parentage (his father was an African-born Muslim). However, as we all know President Obama won the election. At the same time, many Muslims supported President Barack Obama because they felt his election could send a message that Muslims have a place in America. In the end, it seems race and sex issues can be, overcome in this election, but religion, especially Islam, may not be so easily overlooked (Telhami, 2004).

According to Tahir Abbas (2005), discrimination against Muslims in the US has increased since September 11, 2001.

Hostility and attacks against Muslims, both verbal and physical, have increased. Recently there have been numerous press reports of violent assaults and attacks on individuals and property such as mosques. Generally, there seems to be an increase in Islamophobia.

Research has shown that general hostility exists towards Islam and Muslims" (p. 45).

I am writing this new edition for my first book to show how Muslim-Americans are feeling since September 11, 2001. I believe that because of the events 9/11, Muslim-Americans are afraid to vote at polls, because they felt that they would be, discriminated against. My research will investigate this perception. The discrimination did not stop them from voting.

This project has two key objectives: The first objective is to research the challenges Muslim-Americans have to deal with when they try to participate in politics in the September 11 era, especially when they try to vote in the polls. Most Muslim-Americans are afraid to go to the polls and vote. They felt unwelcome and they were afraid of discrimination. The second objective is to educate the public about the challenges Muslim Americans face when they try to participate in politics. Nowadays, the public may make their comments or opinions about American-Muslims, without knowing facts.

My Research Questions:

1. Has the climate of fear inspired by the "war on terror" and the invasion of Iraq led Muslim-Americans to become more engaged---- or less engaged---- in the political process (with a focus on participation in presidential elections)?

2. How do Muslim-Americans feel about the political process in particular the 2008 elections and their ability to have a voice in this process (especially in the 2008 election)?

<u>My Hypotheses:</u>

After initial research on the above questions, I made the following hypotheses:

H1:   I believe that Muslim-Americans will feel they have experienced discrimination since September 11, 2001, when they attempt to vote in person.

H2: I believe most Muslim-Americans will support Barack Obama over John McCain and Hillary Clinton because they feel he better understands their own discrimination (mostly due to the fact that he has a Muslim-sounding name and his experience as an African-American in the U.S.).

H3: I also believe they will probably split in their attitudes about political participation. Half will believe the best response to discrimination is getting more involved in politics (i.e., voting), and the other half will withdraw from politics in response to their perceptions of discrimination.

My Audience:

The reason that I am writing this new edition is to show to the public how Muslims are feeling and what they were going through in election the election of 2008. My ultimate goal is to educate the public (and especially non-Muslims) about the challenges that Muslim Americans face with political participation. For example, in my personal experience, I have found that many Muslims voted through the computer, and through the mail.

They did whatever it took to avoid doing it at the polls, because they had fear of, discrimination or intimidation by poll workers and other voters. Furthermore, this new edition will educate the public and make them aware of what is actually happening around them, to their Muslim-American neighbors.

Chapter 3

How this project is related to my BIS concentration:

My two concentrations, International Government Politics and Administration of Justice are always united. Politics is, based on law; no one can separate the law from politics. Without laws, it is impossible to run politics fairly. In addition, law is what completes politics. The outcome of political action is usually a law. Furthermore, there are laws on how to run campaigns, how to run the polling stations, how to run for a congressional representative seat or the presidency. If you do not apply the law in any of these cases, the outcome is useless, and democracy itself can be, threatened.

My first concentration, International Government Politics were; connected to my project by informing the public about Muslim-American participation. For example, American Muslims face many problems in the US, due to American foreign policies and the wars in the Middle East. The political involvement of Muslims may become problematic with this international situation. American-Muslims are more in tune with the way of negotiating with their fellow Muslims in the Middle East. Perhaps more involvement from American-Muslims could show

Americans other peaceful ways to handle the current wars in the Middle East. Like President Obama is focusing towards the war in Iraq and Afghanistan right now.

My second concentration, was Administration of Justice, and connected to this project as well. With regard to elections, my ADJ courses suggest that all of our candidates should be, seen equally and they should all get proper justice. This will let the voter decide who would be the best candidate for the U.S. In short, Federal-voting law makes discrimination illegal against individuals based on religion, sex, and race.

Background Statement:

The 2008 Presidential elections had many Americans diligently preparing and participating in campaigning to elect a President of the United States. Some Muslim- Americans were also trying to take part in supporting and campaigning for candidates. Muslim Americans had varied views towards 2008 Presidential elections. According to the Pew Research Center (2007), some Muslim-Americans felt that if a candidate has a Muslim background, that candidate will not have an equal chance in the Presidential elections. Other Muslim-Americans felt that their participation may not be, heard because of their religion. Moreover, foreign policy is only one of many issues that concern Muslim-Americans (PEW Research Center, 2007). Still other Muslims in America feel they are, criticized by other Americans, no matter what are in their hearts (Telhami, 2004). In short, many commentators feel that the main problem that Muslims-Americans are facing right now is discrimination, based on their ethnicity and religion (Telhami, 2004). Given this environment of discrimination, one should expect that Muslim-Americans would face problems when they attempt to participate in the voting process, due to their religion. Therefore, after everyone worked hard for the election of 2008, we finally won the victory. Therefore, their participation in the Presidential elections of 2008 was a hard mission. Because of the environment of discrimination, Muslim-

Americans must fight their fear of being, misjudged when they go to vote. As an example, of how this environment affects the political participation of Muslim Americans. Hazem (2008), writes that a majority of Americans would never vote for a Muslims presidential candidate under any circumstances: Though it was scarcely covered by the media, a November 2006 Rasmussen poll found that 61% of [Likely Voters] said they would never vote for a Muslim Presidential candidate. While no Muslim candidate has yet to announce their candidacy, this is hardly encouraging news for Barak Hussein Obama, with Muslim ancestry hanging over his head, as both his father and stepfather come from a Muslim background. (Hazem, 2008). President Obama finally won.

This negativity and discrimination may discourage Muslim-Americans from putting any input into the Presidential elections. In a way, Muslim-Americans feel that they are still paying for what happened on September 11, 2001. The discrimination is still alive, which will never die-down.

Muslim-Americans: Varied Political Views

One, insightful observer of the relations between Muslim Americans and American politics is Shibley Telhami. Telhami (2004), writing in agreement with the Pew Center, argues that Muslim-Americans' views towards the 2008 elections were indeed, varied. Some Muslim-Americans, according to Telhami, believe the U.S. Presidency is for sale. Others believe that "Americans tend to see foreigners as subversives which sexism and racism might be able to be overcome, but not as easily with religion and religious ancestry."

Telhami writes that Muslim Americans are also "sensitive to foreign policy or domestic policy depending upon their status as indigenous or immigrant peoples, who tends to lead them towards a Democratic or Republic stance in the political arena." (Telhami, 2004, pp. 8-12). This variety of perspectives makes sense because, according to the Pew Center for the People and the Press (2007), Muslim Americans come from a variety of backgrounds.

Muslim American:
Who Are They?

	Total %
Proportion who are...	
Foreign born Muslims	65
Arab region	24
Pakistan	8
Other South Asia	10
Iran	8
Europe	5
Other Africa	4
Other	6
Native-born Muslims	35
African American	20
Other	15
	100
Foreign born Muslims	65
Year immigrates:	
2000-2007	18
1990-1999	21
1980-1989	11
Native born Muslims	35
Percent who are...	
Coverts to Islam	21
Born Muslim	14

(PEW Research Center for the People and the Press).

Finally, many Muslim-Americans believe that other Americans see them as a threat since September 11 (Telhami, 2004). In short, Telhami writes that many Muslim- Americans believe that Americans see them as subversives, and that they are always suspect, regardless of their intentions or their contributions to society. As a result, "most Arabs and Muslims today see the U.S. war on terrorism as an attack on them, whereas an increasing number of Americans see Islam as a threat" (Telhami, 2004). These kinds of sentiments can create mutual feelings of ill will.

Perceptions of Discrimination and Political Participations, according to William J. Crotty (2004), "in numerous speeches, the president consistently portrayed the U.S. cause as one designed to enhance the value of freedom, religious tolerance, and a belief in progress, while castigating the terrorist as 'evil doers' who practice 'a fringe form of Islamic extremism'" (p. 47). Yet, many Muslim-Americans believe that other Americans have looked down on them and their religion since September 11. Whenever there is a terrorist attack, many Americans assume that it is a Muslim before they even research and find out who the real attacker is.

Given this environment after September 11, some Muslim-Americans feel that no matter what they do or say, they will face prejudice. Kira Hazem, who is a renowned commentator, has made his own analysis about how qualified political candidates can often face prejudice. Hazem (2008). Hazem, comes up with this conclusion in this manner that: While the country has no official religious litmus test-Article VI of the Constitution states that "no religious test shall ever be required as a qualification to any office"- at the end of the day, voters can, and do, reject candidates based on preconceived notions and prejudice; a classic example of our Democratic system tainted by our habitually Non-liberal tendencies. (n/a).

Hazem is bold enough to make the claim that basically, discrimination against Muslims is a part of the American political process, although it is difficult to prove that these prejudices exist. Others also argue that Muslim-Americans have faced increased discrimination since September 11. According to Bill Ong Hing (2006), "at one point [since] 9/11, hate crimes against Muslims soared, rising more than 1,500 percent. In addition, discrimination in the work place climbed after September 11. So overwhelming was the number of complaints it received that the Equal Employment Opportunity Commission (EEOC) created a new category to track acts of discrimination against Middle Eastern, Muslim, and South Eastern workers after 9/11" (p. 152).

We all know that every religion and every country has good and evil people. We should not see all Muslim-Americans unequally and treat them all like criminals. I have seen my share of this discrimination. For example, I was working in the mall when the September 11 attack happened. A few days later, I was on my lunch break, buying a sandwich. I was dressed in modern clothing, when a Caucasian woman assaulted me. She saw the symbol of God on my jewelry that said "Allah", spit in my face, and cursed me. Even security had to get involved. This is a typical example of how Muslim-Americans are victims of discrimination.

At the same time, how does this environment of discrimination affect the political participation of Muslim Americans? Political participation from all Americans is essential to have a fair and orderly nation. Without participation, injustice and corruption may occur. Politicians need to be, given high standards by Americans so that they act fairly. Recently, the participation of Muslim-Americans since the beginning of the 2008 campaign has increased phenomenally. Hazem writes that this increase in participation has occurred because of Barack Obama's Muslim-American background (although Barack Obama is a Christian, his Muslim background comes from his father, and stepfather). Muslims also participated actively in the 2004 election.

According to a CBSNews.com article, Muslim-Americans Launch Nationwide Voter Registration Campaign, "since September 11, a mosque surveys estimated 750,000 Muslim-Americans are currently registered" (CBSNews.com). Since there was, such a huge number of Muslim-American voters in 2004, there should be an even bigger turnout this 2008 Presidential election (although registered voters do not equal voters.) Still, for a Muslim-American to fully participate in the political activities of their country, they must be, registered to vote and feel support from non-Muslim-Americans. Muslim-Americans need to feel supported by all Americans, because we all live in the United States as well. We all are citizens as well.

Without that support, participation in political campaigns, running for office, or offering money for political campaigns becomes much more difficult. This has been an issue for Muslim-Americans who feel they do not have the support of their fellow Americans; instead, they feel isolated and discriminated against. More specifically, there are many ways that Muslim-Americans may face discrimination at the polls. For example, poll workers and observers may identify Muslim-Americans by the way they dress, their "Muslim-sounding" name, or by noticing jewelry with religious symbols. Some Muslim-Americans have reported that when their names are spotted, at the polls on the voter list, they are screened and their background checked (personal conversations, 2008).

Overall, Americans need to become aware of what is happening to their Muslim neighbors and to condemn the unequal treatment. In pluralist societies, where people of many faiths have agreed to live together in harmony, the Islamic thing to do is to pursue universal values and the universal public interest. To promote the public interest, all citizens must engage in the political process. Khan Muqtedar (2004), who has written on the relationship between Islam and politics, writes that Muslims and non-Muslims should work together to build a healthier democracy. This process will take a long time.

It is important to remember that there will be many more elections to come and Muslim-Americans must not act as if this is the only opportunity they have at making a difference. In the end, Muqtedar writes, "Muslim-Americans must stop having what he calls an "instrumental relationship" (n.a) with the American system. It is time the community went far beyond one or two defining issues (as in policy toward the Middle East), and started engaging the large challenges that America now faces.

Methodology:

First, I did review previous research to gain knowledge about how Muslim Americans view the elections of 2008, with a focus on research articles from academic journals (using database searches like J-STOR). Second, I did conduct an online survey of the views of Muslim-Americans. By using "survey monkey," an online survey research tool, Muslims-Americans can express their opinions about-facing discrimination. At the same time, my paper may help educate those non-Muslim-Americans who may discriminate against them. I first got HSRB approval for my survey. After I got the approval, I did post all of survey questions into the online survey tool.

Then, I did contact most of the Muslim-American organizations nationwide and direct them to the online survey. I also did go to nearby Mosques and asked them to distribute the survey for me to their congregations. I also did use Internet networking tools to reach a greater survey pool, such as MySpace and Facebook.

<u>Conclusion</u>

I believe my survey did show, first, how Muslim-American viewed on the American political situation and agenda and 2008 presidential elections were as far-reaching and as varied as the individuals themselves were. For example, some Muslims believe that the American presidential elections are tantamount to a secret society or club, where only the wealthy can enter and participate (Ramey, 2007). Others have different concerns when it comes to American politics. According Mazrui (1996), although "indigenous American Muslims were highly sensitive to issues of domestic policy in the United States, immigrant American Muslims are more sensitive to the foreign policy of the United States" (n/a).

In addition, I believe my survey did document how discrimination is preventing Muslim-Americans from participating in the Presidential elections or, what is worse, voting November 2008. That did not pose a problem, because Muslim Americans did not stayed home in November, there was not a lack of participation on the election. The Muslim American community is growing. As Mazui (1996) writes, the two sets of Muslims in the United States—indigenous and immigrants—are "in the process of being forged into the largest Muslim nation in the Americas" (p. 493-506). Second, Muslim Americans did vote more for one party than the other did this year.

As Ali Mazuri (1996) writes, "if Muslims are discriminated against or harassed at home within the United States, the Democrats are more likely to come to their rescue than the Republicans" (pp 493-506). In conclusion, Americans still harbor racist attitudes and tendencies. Muslims are feeling the heat especially since the horrible September 11 incident.

Most Muslim- Americans were afraid to go to the polls and vote because they felt unwelcome and were afraid of being, discriminated against.

Introduction to true feelings of Muslims

While, challenged as all citizens to participate in the political system process, in my knowledge Muslim Americans behave as Americans; despite what the polls say or people tend to think about them as a religious entity. Yet, some Muslims in America feel that they are misjudged, despite of the content of their hearts and their true characters. In fact, numerous Muslim Americans believe that the main problem they presently face is discrimination based on their ethnicity and religion. For example, it is definitely amazing

35

that a black man with a Muslim sounding name and Muslim parentage has won the Democratic nomination for the U.S. presidency.

On the other hand, the President Barrack Obama, an African-American Christian, faced questions about his Muslim roots. In other words, there was cause to believe he might not get a fair chance among some general election voters because of his parentage (his father was an African-born Muslim). At the same time, many Muslims support Barack Obama because they felt his election could send a message that Muslims have a place in America. After all the hard work, president Obama finally won. In the end, seemingly, race and sex issues were, overcome in the election, but religion, especially Islam was not, be easily overlooked (Telhami, 2004). According to Tahir

Abbas (2005), discrimination against Muslims in the US has increased since September 11, 2001.

In particular, since September 11, hostility and attacks against Muslims, both verbal and physical, have increased. Recently there have been numerous press reports of violent assaults and attacks on individuals and property such as mosques. Generally, there seems to be an increase in Islamophobia. Research has shown that general hostility towards Islam and Muslims. (p. 45). It stands to reason, therefore, that this climate of fear and intimidation may affect the ability—or the desire—of Muslim-Americans to participate fully in the political process. For this reason, in this paper I want to explore Muslim-American views on the 2008 election. My research questions include:

Has the climate of fear inspired by the "war on terror" and the invasion of Iraq led Muslim-Americans to become more engaged—or less engaged—in the political process (with a focus on participation in presidential elections)?

How do Muslim-Americans feel about the political process in particular the 2008 elections and their ability to have a voice in this process (especially in the 2008 election)?

<u>During The Research Process</u>

While I was conducting library research on my study, decided to use surveys in order to answer my research questions as accurately as possible. To this end, I conducted an online survey of the views of Muslim-Americans regarding the 2008 presidential election. The survey was, designed to measure respondents' intention to participate in the 2008 election (compared to participation in previous elections), their experiences with discrimination at the polls, and their opinions about discrimination against

Muslims more generally. Here are some of my survey questions (for a copy of the full survey, please refer to Appendix A).

1) If you plan to vote in 2008, who would you like to vote for (choose from one of the remaining three candidates)?

2) Have you ever felt discriminated against when trying to vote at the polls?

3) Why do you think Muslims face discrimination in the United States?

After obtaining approval to conduct the survey from George Mason University's Human Subjects Review Board, I recruited a convenience sample of Muslim-Americans, primarily from Northern Virginia, but also from other parts of the U.S. as well. To recruit this sample, I visited local banks that employed many Muslims. I also went to nearby Mosques and asked their leaders to distribute the survey to their congregations.

Furthermore, I used the Internet networking tools, such as MySpace and Facebook, to reach a greater survey pool. Finally, I emailed the survey link to George Mason University students as well. In the end, 164 participants accessed the online survey; 156, participants completed all 15 questions. What I discovered was that my survey respondents felt that this country had treated them wrongly.

Findings

The main reason for the initial questions in my survey was to be sure that participants considered themselves Muslim and that they were at least 18 years old in order to vote in the 2008 election. More than 95 percent respondents who accessed the survey were over 18, and more than two-thirds considered themselves Muslim. If any participants answered "no" to either of these questions, the online survey tool took them immediately to the exit page. As a result, all those who filled out the remainder of the survey were both old enough to vote and considered themselves to be Muslims.

Section 1:
Muslim Political Participation 2000-2008

Table 1:
Did you vote in the 2000 Presidential election?

	%
Yes	31.07
No	63.03
Don't know	.05
Total	100%

Table 2:

Did you vote in the 2004 Presidential election?

	%
Yes	42.04
No	43.02
Don't Know	14.04
Total	100%

Table 3:

Do you plan to vote in the 2008 Presidential election?

	%
Yes	81.09
No	15.02
Don't Know	02.09
Total	100%

My first research question asked if the climate of fear inspired by the "war on terror" and the invasion of Iraq has led Muslim-Americans to become more engaged in presidential elections.

My third hypothesis predicted that respondents would be, split in their attitudes about political participation. In short, I predicted that half would believe the best response to discrimination is getting more involved in politics (and would increase their participation), while half would believe the best response would be to withdraw from politics. The survey results did not support this hypothesis. This sample was; not split. Instead, respondents showed a steadily increasing commitment to voting in American presidential elections. 31 percent of Muslim-Americans voted in the 2000 election, 42.4 percent voted in 2004. However, in the year's election they were truly motivated to vote, with over 86 percent of Muslim-Americans stating they plan to vote in the election of 2008.

As we, all will see it may possibly, be, a single candidate who is conveying Muslim-Americans; to the polls this year: Barack Obama. The astonishing level of Muslim support for Senator Obama and the reasons for this excitement will be, discussed below.

Section 2: Perceptions of Voting Discrimination

My second research question explored how Muslim-Americans feel about the political process—in particular the 2008 elections—and their ability to have a voice in this process, and my first hypothesis predicted that most survey respondents would feel they have been discriminated against at the polls, and would have concerns that their voices would not be heard in the election this fall. The findings that address this question and hypothesis are, summarized below.

Table 4:

When I go to vote I feel unwelcome.

	%
Strongly Agree	36.08
Agree	10.05
Neutral	28.22
Disagree	08.04
Strongly Disagree	16.08
Total	100%

As you can see in Table 4, over 45 percent of the respondents felt unwelcome when they attempt to vote at the pools, while 30 percent no opinion. Only 25 percent of Muslim respondents disagreed with the statement that they feel unwelcome when attempting to vote. This finding is troubling. Since this is a country that promotes democracy and freedom the percentage for the discrimination should be zero.

Table 5:

I feel afraid to vote in this upcoming election

	%
Strongly Agree	31.06
Agree	07.04
Neutral	29.44
Disagree	10.55
Strongly Disagree	21.01
Total	100%

The results were more, equally split between those who feel afraid (almost 40%), and those who do not (more than 30%). While a number of respondents felt unwelcome, this right away translates into fear. Still, more respondents said they were more afraid than unafraid.

Table 6:

Muslims will be able to vote in the 2008 election without being, discriminated against at the polls.

	%
Strongly Agree	40.09
Agree	14.01
Neutral	23.07
Disagree	12.09
Strongly Disagree	09.07
Total	100%

Table 7:

Have you ever felt discriminated against when trying to vote at the polls?

	%
Yes	34.0
No	47.09
I Don't Know	21.03
Total	100%

The results reported in Table 6 and Table 7 show that the majority of respondents, although feeling unwelcome or even afraid, still feel that they will be able to vote without occurrence of obvious unfairness, or discrimination.

Yet, the findings are still troubling. Over one-third of respondents reported that they had faced discrimination at the polls, and close to one-fourth said that Muslims would face discrimination at the polls in November. Ideally, these numbers should be much smaller. We will be able to learn more about how Muslim-American feels about voting and discrimination in America by reading their responses to the open-ended questions of the survey.

Table 8:

Have you ever felt discriminated against when trying to vote at the polls?

	%
Yes	34.0
No	47.09
Don't Know	21.03
Total	100%

What I found was that, as stated above, many Muslim-Americans do feel that they have been experiencing discrimination since September 11th, 2001, including when they attempt to vote in person. Here are a couple of examples of how Muslim-Americans feel discomfort when attempting to vote. One respondent discussed being, treated differently because of her headscarf.

"Because I cover myself with a scarf and I have been discriminated against," she said. "Only because I was covered up, they made me wait at least 30 minutes or more, THEN they allowed me to vote [emphasis in original]." Other Muslim-Americans feel a great discomfort to vote, because they feel they will be seen in a demeaning way. "They check you like your [sic] a criminal," as one participant wrote. Incidentally, this is the one reason why Muslim-

Americans believe that Barack Obama will be the only one to listen to their voices and stop discrimination at the same time. As one respondent said, "Obama...will look at all of us with the same eyes." Muslim-Americans do trust Barack Obama; they all think that he will bring peace and love in not only America but also all around the world.

Explaining Discrimination

Many Muslim-Americans do feel that they have been experiencing discrimination since September 11, 2001, including when they attempt to vote in person. As one respondent wrote, "we are paying for events for which we didn't plan.9/11...we had nothing to do with that." Sadly, many feel that non-Muslims hate them because of these attacks. I will give you two more examples of this. First, one participant wrote, "once I was followed all the way to my home...when I parked my car, the person yelled at me saying for me to go to my real home. I am unwelcome." In addition, the second one is very interesting. I would have never thought that could happen to my any of my Muslim brothers and sisters.

"People walk the other way if I walk by them... they grab weapons to defend themselves...I have no weapon...I can be attacked just for being Muslim."

In addition, some of my participants wrote on my survey that they believe that Republicans make Muslim-Americans look like criminals and make Muslims look bad so the society can hate them **as they do now.** As one participant wrote, "since [a] Republican got in White House...Muslims [have] been hated since." Another put it this way: "Republicans makes [sic] Muslims feel unwelcome." Finally, a number of respondents suggested that the discrimination against Muslims could be, linked to religious differences. In short, many respondents felt their religion was under attack by many Americans since 9/11.

As one respondent said, "they do not even know anything about the holy book Quran, they just make their assumption based on what they believe." Another respondent put it this way: "Americans were trying to mourn and take vengeance on those who attacked the US. However, they are attacking the religion not the people who did it." In response to an open-ended question that asked those participants who did perceive discrimination against Muslims to explain why they felt this discrimination existed, one participant said, simply, "because Americans like to blame everything on Muslims." In response to almost all of my questions, in short, participants talked about terrorism and religious discrimination.

As one respondent said, "Because they all believes [sic] that all Muslims are terrorist, it is like we say all Americans are KKK. They don't make sense." That shows very clearly that many Muslims feel they have been treated wrongly in the United States, and in the end, this overall climate of religious discrimination may help explain the feelings of fear and discomfort that many respondents expressed about voting in person at the polls.

Section 3:

Support for Senator Barack Obama

Table 9:

If you plan to vote in 2008, whom would you like to vote for? Choose from one of the remaining candidates:

	%
John McCain	04.0
Hillary Clinton	03.02
Barack Obama	92.08

My second hypothesis predicted that most survey respondents would support Barack Obama over John McCain and Hillary Clinton because they feel he better understands their own discrimination, mostly due to the fact that he has a Muslim-sounding name and his experience as an African- American in the U.S.

This hypothesis was supported by my survey results.

First, only 4.0% said they would vote for McCain, and only 3.2 percent said they would for Hillary Clinton [note: the survey was distributed during the primary campaign]. A huge majority of 92.8 percent said they planned to vote for Barack Obama. What explains this level of support for Barak Obama? First, it is almost unbelievable to see that absolutely no participants mentioned why they wanted to vote for John McCain, but one participant did say that he or she could not "stand Republicans". For candidate Hillary Clinton only one respondent said, "she is amazing." Nothing more was said about these two candidates.

Yet 119 Muslim-American participants discussed and talked very highly about Barack Obama. They clearly explained why they want him to be the president.

Some participants said that they want him to be the president because "he is the same color as us". Other participants talked about his family background, including his connections to the Muslim community. Since he has a Muslim background, as one respondent put it, "he feels what we feel." Another put it this way: "His Muslim background will make all Muslims vote for him." I must say this individual truly loved him. Many participants also mentioned that Barack Obama would put a stop to discrimination against Muslims. "He gives me the confidence that he will give Muslim-Americans a chance to redeem ourselves as human beings and make a good difference in the U.S." Other participants mentioned the competition between religions in America.

These respondents felt very strongly that there is a big competition between Islam and Christianity, but they also believed that, because Obama has connections to both Christian and Muslim faiths, he "will stop the competition between Muslims and Christians." Many in the sample felt that Barack Obama will stop the religious hate that is going around. The faith the participants placed in Barack Obama can also be, seen in their responses to the open-ended question – what should American Muslims do to prevent discrimination at the polls? Many respondents said that we should simply vote for

Senator Obama "to make sure Mr. Barack Obama wins this election 2008."

Again, most of my survey participants mentioned that the candidate Barack Obama would put stop to discrimination. "To vote for Barack Obama, his Muslim background will help us to be discriminated [sic] free." Muslim-Americans do feel the heat since post 9/11. I believe that no matter what, they still voted in the election year of 2008 for President Barack Obama, because Muslims feel that he will be the only one who can support them to be discriminated free in this country. Obama will "show the world that we are not all terrorists, just like all white people are not members of the KKK."

In several places the participants also said that Barack Obama is the only one everyone should vote for because he is like JFK—the presidential candidate that overcame divisions between Protestants and Catholics in U.S. politics. As one respondent put it, we should "vote for Obama because he is the first true citizen who has campaigned for the presidency...he will make sure that people receive free treatment and their rights fulfilled. He is the next JFK." Muslim-Americans do trust and know that Barack Obama's knowledge will be useful in a way, to stop discrimination and comparisons between religions. Respondents also supported Obama for reasons that had nothing to do with religion or discrimination. They also talk about his kindness and humbleness.

"The world loves his humbleness...and his smartness...we need to be lifted up since Bush ruined the U.S...we are almost like a 3rd world country now." Another respondent also discussed his personal qualities. "I believe that he has the intelligence, temperament, leadership style and ethics to be President; his policies as well as his larger vision of re-engaging American citizens in our country's governance are what we need right now." One last thing the participants truly feel is that Barack Obama is the only one who can bring safety and security in this country: "I believe Mr. Obama portrays a vision of America that has been lost over the last two decades. He portrays an America where prosperity is attainable and our homeland is secure, respected and prosperous."

The participants talk so highly about Barack Obama.

Section 4: Barack Obama and Race/Religious Discrimination

Table 10:

I believe many Americans will vote against Barack Obama because he is an African-American.

	%
Strongly Agree	43.0
Agree	23.07
Neutral	18.03
Disagree	11.08
Strongly Disagree	05.04
Total	100%

Table 11:

I believe many Americans will vote against Barack Obama because he has a Muslim middle name.

	%
Strongly Agree	45.02
Agree	25.08
Neutral	22.06
Disagree	07.05
Strongly Disagree	04.03
Total	100%

As we all can observe, more than two-thirds of participants mentioned that Barack Obama would lose votes due to race and color.

More than 70 percent mentioned that he would not win the vote for 2008 elections because of his family ties with Muslims faith.

What this means to me is that although the respondents are united in support of Barack Obama, they worry that other Americans will not give Barack Obama a fair chance due to racial and religious discrimination.

Wazhma Khalili

Discussion and Conclusion

I believe that my survey showed that the amount of Muslim participation in American presidential elections has improved tremendously. This survey also suggests that, no matter what, Muslims will participate in record numbers in this election year. Muslims will vote even if they feel discriminated against by poll workers or observers—as significant minorities of my sample (between 25% and 40%) did. Muslim-Americans will do whatever it takes to make sure that Barack Obama wins.

I have also learned that Muslim-Americans feel they have faced discrimination in this country since 9/11, and that they have placed great faith in Senator Obama, believing that he will end this discrimination. In the future, I will use this survey to educate non Muslim-Americans in this country and I hope that this will send a message and stop the discrimination. On an immediate practical level, I believe that if state or county officials hire some poll workers who are Muslims, this would be one way to stop the discrimination.

Weaknesses and Limitations

This study was very challenging as there were not enough books, not enough articles or other previous research on this topic. It took days, nights, weeks, and months to find any information about Muslim views. As with most studies, my sample may have biases, which would then take away from the accuracy of my findings. There is not enough emphasis on specific ages and the sex of each participant, which could alter my findings.

For instance, if all the people surveyed were of a specific age, then my sample pool is limited to the opinions of those from that age group; hence, creating inconsistencies in the accuracy of my study. It would have been better to take gender, age and other variables into consideration when devising survey questions, in order to determine if gender or age or ethnicity/national origin affected the findings in an important way. The lack of data about respondents' ages also leads to another weakness, especially with regard to the findings on Muslim political participation. It is possible that the low participation rates of survey respondents in the 2000 and 2004 elections is due to the fact that some respondents may have only recently reached voting age.

Yet, I think this is not the case. When I handed out my survey for example, I gave it to a wide range of ages (not just college students). First, when I went to the mosques with my survey recruitment handout, most folks were middle age. Based on my distribution I believe that more middle age respondents took my survey than those under 30. For this reason I believe the prediction that Muslim-Americans will participate heavily will remain valid.

Future Research

If any one wants to do similar research, they should be very careful as to where to find sources. The new researcher must ask people around for help. Please be advised that this is a very time-consuming project, with lots of reading, writing, and lots of research. Main questions which the future researchers should focus on: · How to overcome the discrimination against Muslims in this country? · What should be done in the area of politics and in law, to prevent discrimination against Muslims? · Do variables such as age groups and gender of Muslim-Americans affect their opinions towards elections? In addition, I recommend to all policymakers to make some changes in their system. The policymakers must hire some Muslims to work at the polls to make Muslim voters feel more comfortable. Also, regardless of who they hire, all poll workers should treat Muslims the same way as they treat other Americans. I also recommend that the employees at polls should be trained well enough before they start taking the vote. Proper training will also help the poll employees to avoid discrimination. If they do not follow their training, they should be dismissed.

Changes occur after the election of 2008:

Right after the election, all Muslim-Americans have seen some changes. There are more job openings, more careers; they receive a lot more respect than before. Discrimination still exists, but not as strong as before. I hope that the research I have done will help many Muslim-Americans and all Americans to understand each other in a better and more respectful way. Thanks to all my audience and readers for their ongoing support and pure love that you have all given me for my book. Once again I greatly appreciate all this, Allah/God bless you all, and protect every single one of you.

Preliminary List of References (MLA):

Abbas, Tahir. Muslim: Communities Under Pressure. London England: 2005.

Avc. Edu, "Administration of Justice Defined." Course Description. Article Date: Unknown, Search Date: April 6, 2008 http://www.avc. edu/catalog/0607-catalog/Administration_ of_Justice.pdf

Bill Ong Hing. <u>Deporting Our Souls: Values,</u>
<u>Morality, and Immigration Policy.</u> Cambridge
University Press: 2006 pg 157

Crotty, J William. <u>The Politics of Terror: The U.S.</u>
<u>Response to 9/11</u>. Northeastern University
Press University Press of New England:
2004.

Journalgazette.Net, "Obama Invokes King
Legacy." <u>Journal Gazette</u>, 5 April 2008.
<http://www.journalgazette.net/apps/
pbcs.dll/article?AID=/20080405/LOCAL/
804050349/1002/LOCAL>

Fisher, William. <u>POLITICS-U.S: Arab, Muslim</u>
<u>Americans Targeted Again</u>. <https://www.

riskinstitute.org/peri/images/file/LP_
dissertationThe_Identity_Of _Crisis.pdf.>

Haddad, Yvonne Yazbeck, and Janel. Smith, and
John L. Esposito. Religion and Immigration:
Christian, Jewish, and Muslim Experiences
in the United States. United States. Lanham,
MD: Altamira Press, 2003.

Kassaimah, Sahar. American Muslims Role in the
Political Process. 16 Feb 2004. <http://
www.masnet.org/views.asp?id=960.>

Liu, Emily. Muslim American Concerns and
Struggles Post 9/11.
<http://www.ithaca.edu/icjournal/02_
muslimamerican.pdf>

Mazrui, Ali A. "Between the Crescent and the Star-Spangled Banner: American Muslims and US Foreign Policy." Ethnicity and International Relations, 72 (July 1996): 493-506.

Pew Research Trust. "Muslim Americans: Middle Class and Mostly Mainstream War on Terror Concerns." 22 May 2007. <http:pewresearch.org/assets/pdf/ muslim- american.pdf>.

Sacirbey, Omar. U.S. Muslims Mobilize in 2006 Elections With Eye on 2008. 31 October 2006. <http://pewforum.org/news/rss. php?NewsID=11751>.

Strum. Philippa. "Conference -- Chicago Council on Global Affairs' Task Force Report on Strengthening America: The Civic and Political Integration of Muslim Americans." 27 June 2007. <http://www.wilsoncenter.org/index.cfm?fuseaction=events.event_summary&event_id=217566

Telhami, Shibley. "Ties That Bind: Americans, Arabs, and Israelis after September 11." Foreign Affairs. 83.2 (2004): 8-12.

"Two Muslim Authors React to Survey of Muslim-American Attitudes Toward U.S." Fox News.com: The O'Reilly

www.ingramcontent.com/pod-product-compliance
Lightning Source LLC
Chambersburg PA
CBHW031257280526
45784CB00004B/1883